New To The Lost Coast

Joshua Butts

ISBN 10: 0-9859191-7-5
ISBN 13: 978-0-9859191-7-7

Cover design: Jana Vukovic

Cover image: Marion Post Walcott, *Copper mining section between Ducktown and Copperhill], Tennessee. Fumes from smelting copper for sulfuric acid have destroyed all vegetation and eroded the land*

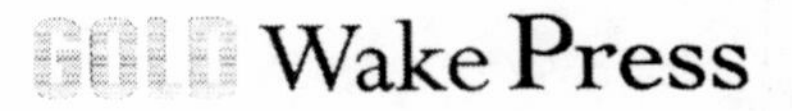

Boston, MA

New to the Lost Coast

for Lesley

Contents

The climate becomes less extreme, the earth grows green and pleasant, human beings and animals are not so fierce. Finally, you come to people living in towns and cities, who are constantly engaged in trade, both by land and by sea, not only with one another or with their immediate neighbors, but even with quite distant countries.

Utopia, Thomas More

The Green Breast

These States

Money for the train and no promise of the landscape reversing—
the land to land rugfest, Berber to barber,
station to station, some ever-present forced farewell.

Hello crazy, hello lovely, hello ugly, hello dire—
how are the folks? Mine were blue. Mine waved.
Mine prayed. Mine begged for one more song.

If I were headed to the highway
which would it be, the road in the distance or the road right here?
Could I get a better answer if I walked a mile?

I've sent out circulars saying I'd be through, announcing
from a rotating speaker the theme of my life—
this by God I'm here for

and I keep going like runners.
If mandolins and trombones collected
I'd request "Sloop John B."

What part of traveling is like collecting rags?
If you've seen a privy the hours in a rented room glow more
than the sunlit kitchen at brunch.

Hollyhocks and flowers await the word to mourn.
The cessation any travel threatens
amounts to popular song.

If you are going to a hotel, you have my blessing
and money for the bath.
If you are going to a church, good luck.

What part of voyage is like collecting the offering?
Roof slats take on rainwater. Ticket takers, faces.
Land is a straight line. Travel is a pill.

Mine bathed. Mine sold arms. There were fifteen here that I didn't know.
Mine saved up coupons to get one of those.
Mine yodeled, then dove into the Great Lake.

Our Ántonia

Cut open the sky
and let the pill bottle

drop through,
a shake sound

as it falls to the twigs.
The bottle finds a girl,

long hair tucked
around a broad face.

Tell us the heart-kill.
Let the blue air feed

at least tobacco.
Your father will

hang the violin
on the wall and then hang

on the wall.
Give us a bib or

a Bible.
Those clothes are flipping

through your brain.
We could crumble thru

pick up some beer.
We could save you

if you were able to stop
the dryer. Most of all

don't lose desire
in a towheaded family.

We are only the blanket.
You are the golden plain.

WPA Poet, 1959

I lost my version of America being content
just thinking color—some kind of refraction,
some jeweled-vision of the self painting the self—
but that was three thousand checkers ago.
Sixteen calendars exhausted and still no devotees—
sound can take its time. What brand of reinterest
could there be (now) for my burgeoning sense of renewal,
for the public as a public, for the early days?
Now: a collection of gestures.
See me, I'm caught in the library
without intention to use the library
though I study cultures of flight and have work to do.
A WPA Poet Will Piddle Around
making lyrics for the latest age.
We'd set on curbs of unbuilt neighborhoods knowing
soon there'd be no nature to capture
yet the flowers in the next field were still as bright
and even then a factory could spur on a subject.
There could have been a poster for anything:
cattle ceaselessly-fenced, horns facing the wall;
bridges crossing even the smaller streams;
golden men and golden shovels trapped in a filibuster.

Blackout

A bicycle
with a raw gear

ticks by in the night.
Sirens like large flying birds

mutter to a measure
odd but regular.

The cream spoils.
Berries hope at least

for a compote.
A collision

tickles from a bumper
a spark so bright.

Fridge on mute—
an emptiness that spooks

and charms.
Chainsaws.

A bicycle with a raw
gear passes.

Henry James wouldn't know
what to do with this

patience and stillness
and boredom.

Write a beautiful line in the middle of the night:
Blackout.

Aging Flâneur

You try to draw a landscape
through dead bushes

or a portrait of a neighbor
cutting the lawn.

He goes back and forth,
clumsy as a dragoon moving into town.

You get up to turn on some music.
He's not getting paid

and when he's done
there will be a dog run through

or a groundhog.
Yesterday a large branch

fell and trampled a minivan
parked in the alley.

You sat out back for a while
and after they pulled it off

went down and
took a quick photograph.

The Green Breast

Looking at the paper I decide franchise
is surely a better word than product.
It's the late days when summer annoyances
cloy and suddenly, "It's too early to mow."
These are hours when laughter is all I catch,
the character actress not yet out with her brood.
Unemployed and nothing but to brood,
I'm forced to think FRANCHISE
or unemployment, some catch
to avoid becoming a product,
spending hours bending handles for some bucket. I could mow
but my shins know the annoyance
a stranger's grass can harbor: annoying
ticks and chiggers, no-see-ums, a brood
that latches while you mow.
And I might be cutting fields at franchises
where they refuse to use products.
Safe at home, sort of. There must be a catch.
From the porch my neighbor asks, "What's the catch?"
There have been glances—do I annoy?
I say, "I treat my lawn with products
of an ordained variety and still this brood
threatens my equity—my franchise."
"Well, why not mow and mow
until the grass is bare to the ground. Mow
your solitary lawn until every last patch
is gone and stitch a single seed so each strand grows *like* a franchise?"
Being lowly and poor seldom so annoys.
I've been trying to keep myself from brooding.
Come by air my blues are purely a borrowed product.

I've hired a starlet to sell sod as a product:
strong wheat, embroidered, set to mow and mow.
No need to stack oil-soaked walls with XXX. No brood
of well-meaning boll weevils are set to catch
worms in the dirt-filled hull. No annoyance.
The seed: FFF (Founding Fathers Franchise).
The blues are a product of no brood—
no calculated annoyance, no franchise
but a person caught for mowing, etc.

Libertarian Lawns

A spate of weeds grows up around the cannon.
Brambles spur through iron

signs. Bumpers hug the asses of the sedans:
Keep Your Government Out Of My Drip Pan.

The signs don't sing of a new America (coal)
but of something clung to, a lull,

a slow bolt riding by on a bike, a gang of kids
walking, wearing ear buds.

They are silent these lawns.
They lack sheep. They lack the munching, the chewing, the yawn.

The structure—if there is a structure—
is like explaining a stir fry, or a detour.

The lawns aren't shorn.
They aren't lawns. But I love them: the furniture gone

wrong like cluttered yards
in Pickletown 1980's:

the only missing thing: coonhounds.
The property owners might trim around

the cannonballs, the placards, though then, of course, then,
the weeds and abandoned

projects would be less free. And the yards
I would love them less.

Bowling Green!

The Defiant Ones (1958)

Send in the hounds
and the sudden rebop radio
in the travel-ready leather pouch.

The movie is old, dead owl.
Cause the decade is old, dead owl.
All languages say "thanks."

Bugs have the manners—
they run when you mute the room.
The landscape is a print.

River water, lucky
not to hit the rocks—
here's where they crossed.

There's machinery—
backhoe, Jeep—
and cons, toads, and coded fawns.

The allegory chases one down.
We are bayonets,
but still the night

can scare us. Catch a water pail
and catch some of that
water—swim, tie a string that will snap.

There's always a village,
a turpentine camp.
Is that Duane Eddy?

There's always a kid,
the man off. Then a convict
gets a warm rag to the forehead—

healing after all is healing—
that it is started
it is done. His savior is a soft focus

stranded lady
born twenty miles
and don't know a thing.

There's always a car
that won't start
and then it starts. Always a farewell.

Pick up quick, to Canada,
looking out for Mounties.
The convicts don't always get caught,

are usually shot.
Bowling Green! Sewing Machine!
Desperate, joyful.

The Funeral Hat

Trade a scam for an uneven dollar
and you'll pay it back double,
said the man in the shirtsleeves.
Dandelions were burning
like cartoon cigarettes
out the window of the traveling bus.
I knew that night I could blow smoke
through the hotel room transom
and somehow escape
the wind of the miles
but that hour was long off and running
away couldn't get me
far enough into the scam
and I had no scam to pull.
I had been living life cleanly,
each morning practicing the military
tuck. But this man kept promising
a lozenge, a change in temperature.
He had a nasty cut on his lip.
I asked him when he sat down, Are you alright, Sir?
He said it was an old wound
and that I should see the knife.
Bruised sidekicks are easy playmates
but this man was a stranger and his
chatter was becoming more and more profuse.
His mother had memories of the Crimean War.
I felt that couldn't have been possible
we were riding on a bus.
He told a story about a young girl drowning.
He and a cousin were at a picnic

migrant workers, vagrants really.
Bastard that I am, I hadn't heard of the Crimean War
and thought for an hour of the blackness
of the night. It was like this new thing
they talk about—noir film. I don't like Robert Mitchum.
We are the same age. I think he looks like a wooden box
trying to have a conversation with a baby.
He's rough. He splinters. I don't think women
would give him a glance but then
they might lie if I brokered an opinion.
In every hotel bar I get the shut up and go to sleep—
but that's because I'm fat. I wait until the next day
but then I eat, forking my way.
I'm too young to feel that wheels are fictional creatures.
They speak to me like the whining score in a melodrama.
The strings bring the sun up—
in the theatre it would be strings.

Movie Afternoon

If you could purchase a pony with a whine so quiet it rarely defined
the silence it deafened, what a feat for the L.A. streets
where there's no ordinance for a monkey or a steeplechase.
The stable life out here is unstable.

In this scene a salesman tries to introduce the Napkin, but the extra
with the paper wipe appears colonial and this is not a way-back-there
picture. The actors disassemble, but the dinner will be the same small
boxes releasing chicken vapor into crumpled paper.

A competent moon hangs above the lunch carts and sodas.
Blue mountains ferret a yellow sky as imperceptible backstory tempts
gin hand-to-hand under the red checkered table cloths. (Could you pass
the biscuits?) The writer says: Let them hurt themselves.

We will film the afterlife hardboiled. The producer says: It won't shoot.
There was always to be a girl jumping rope. She'd wear chartreuse—
and there'd be that bit of fishing and the sky would be day-like,
but the land wasn't to fall onto itself and into the water.

Rodeo Ramble

The Misfits (1961)

Mustanging, you misfit!
You've broken your arm, your clavicle.
You sold your heart at the bottom
of a square bottle.

I have an onion, you have a pain.
Your bruised back is puffed
pastel orange egg crate.
The phone booth is empty.

Your cord is cut, tubular
flap through a dark heaven.
Heath. Whisky snore.
A bend around the mime barrel.

The heart reports joy.
He gets skiffle about his ritual.
He tugs his loops, clicks his jaw.
He has a lot of grit, a lot of try.

Oscilloscope charts the wave
of the rippled beast's back.
A beggar can wrestle sixty head,
can make a stock of the mane,

can sell the bones to giants
if the rope ripples silver.
Street sausage. Oil. A drink
to near death. Mustanging!

The airplane man wants to try.
Blond breasts, starched collars.
You misfit! I want off.
I want back on.

Alaskan Abecedary

America in the middle
of autumn and the amateurs
are fallen.

Begin and tell me
what things
are effusive enough.

Call out
to the excuse
for Alaska.

Devil the youth
along the path of school
and into country living and grow only adults.

Executors

falling from one
floor to another

in a darkened elevator.

Forty cabins
gone for good

like a compulsive loser's loser at checkers,
loans starving already-garnished food packing wages.

Hope is the drag.
Hope is a drag.

Hope heals.
Hope like a harpoon
hurts.

Iditarod.

Just a few truculent
jonquils to cheer

any summer knit wit

caught in his undies
behind a stable

kept tidy
by some
Katarina,

lovely one
come from the hills
to suffer fools,

lost among a strain of longing
for a landscape   to break a lull between
Roman columns and cigars.

Musher's life is on the trail—

so my cabin *don't worry*

can be small—though never

without feeding and mushing

and feeding and mushing—every

barking day a cycle.

Out there the sound of car trouble—
could be a mother

or some fool trying to find another way
to drive.

Plowers on break from constant plow
bag ptarmigan for dinner and fun:

"Quit! Could you quit?"
asks James when Elvis has killed more than five.

Recalling the first winters
Katarina knew she would miss the red
shake of morning on the Alaskan ice.

South, pilots in small skiffs
net a few salmon
and so find forgetfulness

but Tom
tossed from his last Alaskan apartment
receives a telegram from a friend:

Tom, get here. Catch the rail.

Under the Great Plains
grows an unctuous earth,
and for much

of it, an
underground
sea.

Vast reaching is a rosy
phrase. Track
by track is torture, a vast torture.

What Tom wants is to win the match
where he lives once more,
crossing corner to corner

from X into Y, whole grain and lonesome,
fed or unfed—
knowing with a kiss

to tarry less,
exclaim little
and travel lean.

The York Peppermint Patty
thinks it's cool.

Yes.

The zoologist
has no knowledge
of the loneliness of the polar bear,

and penguin
and otter
and seal.

Harmonica

Take that lion into your mouth
paths that draw to parade and to morning,

morning caught
as if in some interview.

Why do you dwell? I like it. Why do you leave? I go.
Why return? It's really nice here.

The building feels jubilant, random,
a little like a cattail.

Rooms and rooms are having parties
but only that kind of party, one stacked on the other—

they are doing this and we are doing this
and between concrete floors the dancing ends

with a single ring and a single buzz.
Wake up late and play it again.

You can sell a harp but not resell.
Keep telling stories and when you draw

cut it short and resist thinking it's nice only here.
In many places there's still plenty of wildness.

The Ap.

(James A. Rhodes Appalachian Highway, southern Ohio)

Ascendancy

Perspective can do its thing anywhere,
doesn't depend on the scene.

A common snow-cast backyard
projects into the fence and through a valley

you've never noticed
until apprehended

by its pure and unmolested coat.
Adams County Hopewell said

we couldn't know the land.
So we excavated their mounds

and through all the digging
what did we find?

Play set, tool shed, and trees—
slats in the back over ditch, planks so

regular they are destined for paneling.
A welfare line so hard to get through

with the food stamps and all the judging.
So much future they couldn't have predicted

us, the true us, with handkerchiefs,
candles, and very effective draw bridges.

We have been here forever.
It's just we've never seen ourselves

against a blank screen
quite like we have now

with all the beauty a young girl
could ask for, so much she could be sold

for her dynamic face
and her complacent ability to coo,

though she carries a note that says, I can only love you
if your father owns land.

Measley Ridge Road

Moving with the weather is no option
for those on Measley Ridge.

No vessels are prepped
for when the Brazos sweeten.

Shirley Hughes, send your laundry water
to the nearest stream.

Ziplocs huddle the deaths
of the holiest white poor

with their ragged white meat
and dry bushels

requiring so many creamed sides.
If this were Louisiana

one might know how to make love.
Here they keep waiting on the red pig

to make them all that money.
Find a novelty and something is on.

It gets to be Sunday.
There's supposed to be a reunion

the message moves through the family,
phone to phone, telling the outskirts not to show.

The forgotten played-out orphans
pushing the long boats out into the lake

can get lazy in their tans.
There's no reason to travel to Measley.

Chenoweth Fork Road

Take me down Chenoweth, across Sunfish creek
and we could take off our shoes and place our feet
in the cold, cold. Take me down Chenoweth
and we'll hope the water hasn't risen over the road
and we can make it to the covered dish. We could help
cut that big field of grass. Take me down Chenoweth
and sooner or later we'll get to Poplar Grove,
end up near Smoky Corners, Grooms, Arkoe,
or back near Bacon Flat or Pine Gap,
or over to Duke, Hatch, Lad, or Latham.
(Of course we'd cross The Ap. a few times
and wouldn't really be lost.) Or we could
chase our way to Sinking Spring, trying to find the water.
We could go down Chenoweth to the Pine Bank Boer Goat Farm
and check out the spotted breeding program.
They start kidding soon. Take me down
to the Pine Bank Boer Goat Farm
and we'll check out sires and dams:
bucks and does by War Chief and Cruel Girl,
Rhubarb and Ruby Begonia,
Egg Ryal's Magnum and Sasquatch,
Shanghai Red and Pine Bank Thelma,
Mason Dixon and Pine Bank Paint Spot,
Bosque Valley Sharif Demetrius
and Wiltshire Farm's Bubbles. Take me down Chenoweth,
we'll run along the whole way, singing songs—troubadours.
We'll saunter up to the meal held in a garage—
miles of casserole and grace before we eat. We'll look
for a church and a graveyard. We could have our picnic.
You bring the wine. I'll bring the deviled eggs.

Surely we can find a tree to Watteau under.
Take me down Chenoweth—we can locate high stakes bingo
or carryout video poker. Take me down Chenoweth
this guy I know out there deals in feathers.
He's got whole birds, three for a dollar.

Burnt Cabin Road

You wonder what happened there.

Tranquility Pike

A flash across the windshield at late day
or in the morning can make a wreck.

So if you drive here try to be as patient
as a cat waiting for a door.

You know you are helpless.
Last winter I was covered up—snow

for three weeks can dazzle. The kettle
whirred for coffee until I ran out.

I lived on tomatoes cooked quick with salt.
(We are pure blood around here.)

I'm not lonely. Heat and rain breed many weeds.
I've been sober as a bell at midnight—

is that a phrase? My talk show host has been gone,
captured in fact. His band plays a familiar waltz

and then it's morning, the heat swallows
the valley, soaks the blacktop, rises

like a camphor from the road and so I wait
on this rain and then it pours and pours.

It hits in my head and I tell myself,
This isn't the kind of rain that answers questions.

Could I take my wrong moments,
set them to some tune? If you need flannels,

I'll send you a bagful.
Give them to people you meet under street lamps.

Tater Ridge Road

The orange paint: two rooms.
Every Wednesday and Sunday we church.
Among the rescued we recognize the wrong done.

We don't build boats but deal
in golden and gracious praise.
If there is song, we check the song.

We allow song—any song, any beat.
For some our rules are too rough.
For some our rules are not enough.

If there are spirits, we drink them.
If there are not, we rattle drums
and wait on the spirits.

There may be hours and hours of footage proving otherwise,
but we know which tree to hang our clothes on
for the super-dry.

Coal Dock Road

Catching the Pennsylvania to Chicago
I knew you were up to more than a smokehouse.

If I'd captured your voice in some small tin can
then all this papered-light wouldn't so upset.

The buckets near the coalhouse haven't moved
and winter is near so if you favor poker

there are cards here in the dark and heaven is greedy
so hurry. If my feeling seems forest-bound

let me unknot. Our bedroom is high, a-level
with the poplars. There's a wind that blows

through the windows. The stones in the creek
are close enough for any fool who needs a weapon.

Here I am your functioning voluptuary—
I hear the hibiscus taking her dream down,

tiny red filters dropping to heighten the feeling
of doubt. I can't mourn your far off avenues.

Get here as quick as the car goes.

Red Hollow Road

With lights like lights
for the biggest coon hunt

Jim White's Pinto chases
a fox to the end of the bridge.

No arctic foxes on Red Hollow
except for trips to Beaver

for a euphemism. The wild
out here are to be trusted.

Far out here isn't that far out.

Cars parked forever
under crab apple—the car bivouac

the preferred concert
and the bellies ache all night.

There's a stage near
the backhoed shooting range.

In the scalloped land
the dreadnoughts are strung

to the peculiar note
of the afternoon—

some have fires,
some have brittle fingers.

The grass is sprinkled
with flowers of blue, purple, yellow, and pink.

The deputy for beauty
in the county will be rewarded

with warmth in the morning,
coolness in the afternoon.

His Jeep—bright orange
blasting from forest to water—

kernels, seems ready to sprout.

I've brought the most insulting side dish.

Deer season done,
Christmastime, rural yards

become cities, roads turn safe.
Through the night

tears adjust themselves,
lights get turned on.

The tailor needs an extra button.
The actors disassemble.

The commandments are simple.

When the pauses between
arrows reach twelve minutes

eloquent young men from town
play a stretch of country music.

Then more arrows fly
and after three callers

trim the turkey boxes
the cancellations begin.

Too many roads,
too much wallpaper to hang.

In the morning
the war is over

so we cram our homes
into cars and follow

the customary gestures of daylight.
One highway sign seems to read:

Come lovers to the Cone Zone,
we've got a chill

and so many children show up
the cinema offers

free matinees.
On screen a man

with a horse called Banjo
says, Bring a covered dish.

The silver vat baked beans
are traps of wiles and wiles and wiles.

Remember me when I become a soda.

Union Hill Road

Expanse: room here,
never so high,
near the low Serpent hill.

> Interior: brother string lines,
> quilt, sock,
> quilt, sock, nightmare.

Expanse: arbor beltway,
ear pressure, wire weed train,
oak, smoke, oak.

> Interior: television,
> cable box,
> dust on wooden spoons.

Expanse: tire pressure, hum, and wind,
a steeple here somewhere,
a cellular vacuum.

> Interior: chilly, pepper jelly,
> couch, hutch, broom,
> painted tiers.

Expanse: arbor beltway,
all creatures
fresh and nostalgic.

Interior: city, city, city,
city, city,
city, city, city, city.

Expanse: top of the hill line,
shades lighten
with distance and rain.

Interior: collapsed,
restored to wind,
pre-nostalgic.

Expanse, expanse, expanse.

Tennyson Road

Nearly as beguiling as that town called Academia
Tennyson Road forces brother to brake for a photo.

It isn't cold enough for a jacket and so I
don't have a jacket. I could have used shades.

There was gravel, mud. The pose will be forgotten
in the can as the tender copse to be cased by explorers

calls us passersby. A blueness. Some crabapple.
We drive over the low rise, looking for the blue shack.

No sign of a business we are greeted by a buzz cut.
We pluck five dollars from Velcro wallets and sign the waiver

life, brother, pursuit of happiness. A guide hikes us up the electric-
lined ski slope. For the length of the tour, she says:

These lines stretch to feed cities that are not here.
The grassy, weeded path is a straight cut for a whirligig

but for the towers. We stop near the top as the wind
freshens. I taste sweet spuds and quail and make up a lie

about a market. I would peel the potatoes and stuff
the quail with thyme, maybe fig. My brother

doesn't hear the crackle, thinks the wildflowers
are new and blazing all on their own

Hackleshin Road

Searching for jobs in Latham, the first thing is soldier. No plan for no Pepsi it seemed I'd remain pure Hackleshin. Smoky corners, pines. Then like a bluesman to the old changes I took my tuning fork to Georgia and on. No potato chip had ever felt fear in Latham. The worst I'd done was cut my hand on a tire rim. The white oak of course had something to say. The Kentucky love affair—long-separated—gave a kiss at the gate. Meretricious and handled by the storm, the land never felt my resistance—no buzz to its spark. Devilish perhaps, I made a note of the coordinate: a land without sentimentality on the way to a land without sentimentality. Hackleshin seemed a shabby distance. There was no movie ambition or dalliance. I was a soldier, if stumbled to, an aspiration undefined and there were no trees—no trees. I didn't think of Hackleshin until there was this whinesome sound of I swear a flute. The 40's movie was asleep in his bunk when I plucked the note from my flak jacket pocket and read: "Losing a single toe in a big war silences any crowd." The next morning a red wind settled in as we drove to shoot our guns toward the garden.

Zahn's Corner Road 

Drive above the houses
tucked below the road line and scatter

a momentary tire hum—
watch the hairpin and don't get distracted by

the eroded and ribbed with rebar
castaway gravel

home to an early 80's Pepsi can.
Zahn's Corner has crazy concrete.

There are weeds, weeds,

and a rail bridge's gray stretch
where you learn Wally ♥ Jan.

Throughout the winter dawn
and the winter morning

the hermit notices aspirin
have an actual taste.

Light hits ice under the fence
and there is apple in the whisky.

A clothes hanger catches
the noon news from Cincinnati.

Due to tragedy a young woman argues,
You will hear of every city.

In this case it's Peebles.
There's a flattop on the sexton

who steers the cars.
We'll do this as respectful as we can.

A niece wants a ring off a dead lady's hand.
She has a right.

A store nearby presents a stability
like ashing cigarettes

into a bowl and tomorrow
to wash the bowl and to eat oats.

Many things give pleasure, stimulate
the teeth, the tongue, the gums.

You can get at least one of these
on the wooden floors

of the Zahn's Corner Market:
betel nut, cocaine, Anbesol,

creosote, milk, lotto.

A holler over a hamper claps
as a frazzle-haired teenager

learns the laundry—
mildewed towels

that have never seen a beach,
socks, briefs, a diaper.

He gives up, breaks for a cigarette
on a pure products porch,

a class picture of
bicycle, kickball, tire,

cash register, rust-covered industrial bolt
never recorded.

One Sunday a sculptured surprise of ice cream
depicting southern Ohio

is for sale from an orange igloo cooler,
the kind road crews

use for drinking water.
Stranger treats have come

from even barer spots
but few coated in a chocolate ganache.

Here come the cameras.

Zahn's Corner
leads to the Goodwill.

Spend three dollars
on a black bag of clothes.

Buy another bag
when the clothes start to smoke.

The cable crew films historical
mannequins on North Market

then strums a string
at Prussia Valley Dulcimers.

The Butter Girls strike business
and the Emmet House reopens

so the folks can get prime rib,
baked potato, and a salad—

so the folks can get a salad.
The bar pours a frontier whisky

for the filming crew. Hollywood!
(I think they are from Pennsylvania.)

In the moonlight
just off Zahn's Corner

the spelt sways and rattles
so the fuzzy earth seems to move

into the sky like a song.
But it's something

about junk or love
arranged in that Tulsa sound

and Tulsa blues, tonight, seems so
Zahn's Corner.

I wouldn't lie about
how something is spelt.

The paper struggles to translate
the documentarian's vision:

I'd like to go closer than genus
and species. The Barbary Lion is extinct

though I've spent the night
tracking one on the banks of the Scioto.

It will be a two week project, looking for
the autumnal turn the trees take in October

though the film crew can't escape
the road noise that *hovers and hovers.*

The shack roof clatters with rain,
but there is song:

Emerson bowled me over.
Thoreau cooked my beans.

I have a plan to cut a cut
into the land, to pave a cow path

and unravel the American dram.
I will found a team on Zahn's Corner.

Disc up the earth, paint the lines.
Call the team, The Trains.

Cove Road

Cuddly in your sound branches make you
over, clayed ditches salamander but this

is no trash party or pill-headed crisis.
Cove-roaders invade the area with Cokes

and soothe the locals but the ditches
are treacherous on their own through the

deepest most natural woods. Pick a driveway
and the dead get up and go home.

There are fields in all directions.
No fire can be lit until the pine settles

and they sing of the carbureted land
and the flames curl like the graffiti

for that failed band issued for Detroit
that proclaimed *this one can sing!*

But all along it should've been about
Cove Road—though Cove Road wasn't yet

the lonely brilliance on the terrain
that could attract him, her, until it's all over.

Smokey Hollow Road

I'll drive back to see if I catch
the slow bastards, get a postmark.
The chickens will be home from school after three.

The brown plastic surrounds the staggered
white rectangles in a kind of numbness. The letters
are still on the back seat.

I might give a few dollars to Father Flanagan.
I'll have to get another stamp.
I will lick it in the parking lot and drive to the slot.

I've spent my money on an Eric Clapton cassette.
I've given my teeth over to cavities.
I've sold the Telecaster.

The letters are still on the back seat.
The stamp runs away from the father.
I know what you expect when you go to a museum.

I know what you expect when you avoid laundry.
The letters are bruised white rectangles
sucked by anchored slots at the end

of an empty hallway lined with corn silk
when it should be apple cores
when it should be soft cider.

Shyville Road

e-mail is oyster something
and letters addressed Dear State Fair Dog Agility Participant

find their way through the mail
to mint highway signs that announce

a silver spinning budding aquaculture—
spawning pools, tadpoles, cruel young life

a rifle's bullet from American Centrifuge.
American Centrifuge?

Woods cede to farmland
and the State University extends

operations to include aquaculture
and among so many farms.

Take a right at Wakefield Mound, then a left
at Nursing Home, or just take Shyville.

You can huddle spawning pools right up to it?
Man can make the biggest machines

for the biggest problems
that call for the biggest solutions.

Can there be a county-sized, steam-filled iron
and some wealth of fabric to press

the perfect poor person's uniform for hiring day?
Any need filled. Any? Most.

What was this wiped out town called?
My wife's forebears had a habit of naming communities

after themselves. Here's a print:
Lester Shy on his horse, Custer,

captured by a Brownie No. 2. Photography, 1910
not hot to trot, but *stationary* boy!

The swish of the tail is fuzzy, the only imperfection.
Spoiled by our slicing shutter speed

there are fewer hallucinatory ground up cigars,
the kind of toke that could carry you a mile

to some bandied about bridge where to cross
you have to take a stand on local politics.

But what if you don't know the area?
Assess quickly, or guess. Let the 18-wheelers ride

with the Amish. Then mutter Shyville,
Martin Marietta, A-Plant, aquaculture.

There's the story in the news of the two brothers
waiting for a relative to die, driving country roads

always pining for the opaque serving tray.
Glass can tear folks apart. There are a few people

who remember Shyville? Yes. Lester's sister.
She would've remembered.

Her true Penelope was Beaver Creek.

Gravel Washer Road

You ever had a nightmare, Johnny,
some barn all stuffed with Charolais

and the asphalt cracks a chasm
before each driveway so the stranded

country families feel encased
and subject to the broadcast?

They feel beavercreeked not seeing
lovers, but these may be the days

when the six year olds are forced
to the question of *gravel* and *washer*,

though *road* is far off, resplendent, another country.
The rabbits mock the shooting sets—

everything will freeze. One fall, I wrecked there
when delivering charcuterie.

I'd hitched my cart to a sheep
cavalcade but had trouble

finding my way back to home
as some white jet was haunting.

Black Hollow Road

It's quite bright on Black Hollow,
not the sharp
                    pale mornings,
the impetuous glow under trees.

Fogs are known to camp here—
fogs are not here.
                         A bright morning light,
some plagiarized noon.

The county is confused by changing
mail routes,
                    the dusk too early.
Is there Coffee Hollow envy,

Smokey Hollow?
                         You'd never know
for there's always a cadenza
in the barely pale eve.

New to the Lost Coast

Prehistory

Out of the way upended cars cast the scrap yard
a full but lonely place—frosted bumpers, winter blue light

swelling from chassis and bodies no longer trotting
the cocktail circuit. From this nearly nighttime scene

a figure appears, a man on duty for kids who want a coin
for a bean can. He must have heard my bicycle across the rocks.

I follow him into the office, better than a shack, but with sheetrock
put up without need for a finish. A headline

on a wrinkled stack of newsprint reads: Snowplow Driver in Hot Water.
The watchman resembles that old snob in town

but gives me three dollars for a bag of railroad spikes.
I hear a radio turn on. He doesn't seem to hear it.

Out the window the sky fades brightly in angles
cut oddly sharp like deserters through a field, like ice

cutting down the windshield of an early eighties sedan.
Somewhere out there is an early eighties sedan.

In this scrap yard a few characters will die. Cars will pass.
There are no shots this time. It's that a few are bound to die

on every spot. There are fallen prints abroad and in the next room.
The one to die over this land could be this man paying me in quarters.

State Route

There might be a death mask in the works,
plying oneself with Lightnin' Hopkins.

The only solid words may be piano:
"The Rocky Mountains, Darlin,

they are way out in the west."
I'll take the three-note stroll and get out.

The garden seems a meager thing,
but yesterday the plant produced its first

and everyone spread butter over crusty bread.
The vine, sneaky animal, isn't really a vine.

You need a ladder for a cucumber plant.
Let the zukes lay under the canopy.

Serve dinner and like cancellations after a storm
the creep will be depleted—

fruit by fruit, aubergine by aubergine, spray
by spray, fluke by fluke. But there's no

grid imposed. No almanac with notes
on the availability of corn, legumes, peppers,

bunches of herbs. The only solid words may be
stone fruit. Peaches are smaller

this year. Busking in the garden
means someone will hate you as you bun up

a pile of barbecue. The rungs start to break,
trashing the scaffolding.

The world closes
in a green, viney array.

Sandy Denny

died the day before I was born.
Her parents' stairs were stitched
with fizzy orange carpet, tufty
frayed knots that glowed in the hall
not as if the carpet were near a shore
but just under hall light. She nearly titled
a record *Slapstick Tragedies*. The title
became apt but was likely born
while having a smoke on a shore
wearing some deep winter sweater stitched
from countryside sheep, their tufts
making a perfect grey spool hauled
off and dyed orange, red, not a subtle hallway
color like light brown. The record title
reflects the unspooling of that tuft,
offers a life that should never have been born
into this world without a stitch:
'68 hippies running on a shore,
now tailored Macintoshes living off what's shored
in a box at the end of a hallway.
Are you a traditionalist? "Not a stitch,"
she might've said. "We do ancient titles,
but with the feeling of being born."
Nor did she say, "I don't give a tuft."
This could be verified by a scholar at Tufts
or you might travel shore to shore
to find record of her birth,
trace the inventory along some ancient hallway
sleeved with novels, some rare titles.
Forever really is hipster toile stitched

with Naugahyde squares stitched
to denim, faux fur, and tufts
then printed on covers of long-player titles
from English and L.A. shores.
My favorite Fairport might be "Carter Hall."
Here it is: from virginity a child is born.
But that wasn't the title. Not a stitch
of this is true. It was "Tam Lin," the line: "Carterhaugh."
But there *was* a shore covered in grey tufts.

Retrospective

The sound of ancients
through modern equipment:

the LP a form
on the rungs of the 45, an unbroken

sequence, a level of attention
never forced through the reeds

into the mind—
a note, a squeal, a crowded compendium.

Live on the date from 1888
for chickens, weather.

Devil sightings: 1951, 1966.
Sand dance, 1919.

Collection of
Brandywine tomatoes, 1977.

You can't keep the cannibals away—
seed gatherers picnics,

envelope collectors filing parties.
They give up and roll around

in some grass and flip the manila
until it means the immediate proximity of sky

is an approximation of heaven.
For a young woman, the hunger of cooking

while listening to Fairport Convention,
living long enough to see culture

sense a burn from a bulb
not yet cracked through this green and secure earth.

Then there's the *character*
of the egg farmer, the can man, the car dealer

that cancels all swell complaints.

Poem of the Teenager

Are there strings on the canary and black? If so,
it's hush on the defense. Bruises await the cold tub,

though they are hardly bruises yet. Having come up
with the ball and having broken the plane we go

to the cold millimeters: an older director cutting to the jaw line
of some brute ingénue as she crosses tomboy into straight cut

above the knee organza, still some part of herself
but better, improved, realized. Many films are made on this rule,

plastic high school welcoming puberty by the hand
and welcoming all but those Jan & Dean deadly curves.

Class of '96

Travis is a housepainter.
Stanley works at the hardware.
William works there with him.
On Wednesday they unload nails.
Elkington moved to New York
to act and write and direct.
Clifford misses Elkington.
Elkington misses Clifford.
Benson is a mechanic.
Allen is a mechanic.
J.J. is a mechanic.
They all love carburetors.
James White is selling Bibles.
Hope works at a nursery.
Patrick is in the Marines.
Melody married Henry.
Henry is recalcitrant.
Christopher now tugs a barge.
He used to sell crystal meth.
Merle and Ken do lawn care.
Jennifer is a lawyer.
Victoria takes X-rays.
Jerome plays the piano.
Eddie, Mark, Levon, and George
sell homeowners insurance.
Mark also sells Life and Flood
on the side—George, only Life.
Ann is involved in 4-H.
Cleveland works in a foundry.
Jill, an archeologist,

still finds time to play the drums.
Yoshi moved back to Japan.
He lives in a small tin can.
Eloise is a teacher.
Mary Lou is a teacher.
Katharine, Cynthia, Kate,
Brandy, Jenny, Dot, and Jan
are all substitute teachers.
Jason and B.J. coach ball
and cover P.E. duties.
Zachary sells mobile homes.
Oliver engraves tombstones.
Somewhere out in Idaho
Mike and Brett are both preachers.
Dominique is a dancer.
Hube sells shoes at Less is More.
Holly, Margie, Maggie, June,
Cassie, Molly, Hannah, Clare
and Judy are all housewives.
Grace adopted a baby
from a Russian agency.
Skip is a missionary.
He spent six years in Haiti.
Lucy and Lucy sell wine.
Toria did time for theft.
Lewis, Manny, and of course
Alex have all passed away.
Mario is a draftsman.
Ántonia is a chef.
Evan sells stationery.
Herb and Alice drive box trucks.
Todd, an apprentice plumber,

back from New Orleans last year,
gave up on his dream of jazz.
Marty paints homes for Travis.

Eye-level Lake

Each corn stalk passed charts on the unfathomable
number of corn stalks passed in a middle west life.
Then there are kernels and silk and that's how you define infinity.

Addiction always insists on the present tense
of something that depends upon past and future.
One summer our family visited a state park.

We disguised ourselves as other families who spend
all their time in state parks, though we knew
no family spends all their time in state parks.

Still the marshmallows and lily pads belonged
to us and the lake was so calm that it felt perishable
and the sunscreen and snacks made us infinite

and eternal. But we were infinite and eternal already—
looking for that lost butter sizzling-out on the campfire.
Our rickety pull-behind was always poorly parked.

We never rented the canoes, but paddleboats.
Don't rent the paddleboats, get the canoe.
Row, not paddle, if you hit the lake.

Even if your kids are losers. Even if the kids dip under—
that's what life jackets are for. In the gray glow, in the turn on,
in the boring orange of the fabric, life jackets

in appearance, in bulk, in strapping—connote the past.
Just as *2010* could never be more futuristic than *2001*—
you couldn't imagine the wood involved—

a transport could be made of wood. Here we go—
Bob Ballaban, John Lithgow—so assertively, so
belligerent without fear of the future because of the past.

The composer settles on a saxophone solo.
No blindfolding, no bitterness—all eye-level, all space,
all time, no binary, one brittle feeding cake.

A Long Nap

Yes it feels like a Sunday and *The Goodbye*
Girl is on again—something to sleep to,

to take like some casual vitamin, the way
a piece of shell skates away in the egg

like you can never shoot that gun in the dream.
It gets to be my birthday and my previous version

ensures I spend a gerrymandered ticket
on a central city morning alone thinking "sandwich."

Happy in the basement of the museum,
in the bookstore with the square glossy art books

nudes and racecars—I'm picking out the notes
of some long forgotten theme.

So I go to church to celebrate the red five coming up
and I'm able to order the lunch meat.

All room for new when a young hullaballoo—
but that was a long year still, and what is offered

is clearly Richard Dreyfuss and those brunettes,
ten and thirty-three, respectively.

Benevolent Year

We should feel good that in the future
we will be getting some of our money back.
When the dollars pad the purses it will feel invented

and quietly richer we'll wait for the slap
from the big hand. But the sea will be calm.
Chet Baker is always the music in a benevolent year.

Cameras are never prisons in a benevolent year,
but only shortcuts to the future
when years might not be so benevolent, so calmly

considering your flaws and patting on the back
your triumphs (it *is* a pat and not a slap
so the sting feels invented.)

The year semiconductors were invented
was not the International Geophysical Year
though Velcro, widely promoted hoop and loop, is a slap,

a way to do and un- in the future.
But there is no shame asking for your money back
if the technology doesn't make you calm.

These days you seem more calm.
You barnstorm less. Is it the invention
of the weekend, which feels new, not back

there in that first of benevolent years
when it finally didn't feel like the future
was made of the next moment's slap?

Instead it truly felt like a slap.
There is time. Here it is. You should be calm.
But then the broken tooth of the future

requires dentures and a new embouchure must be invented.
You finally have money. In a benevolent year
folks learn that you are not an asshole

as once thought. You are never an asshole.
Nor are you the kind for the winning-round slap.
You won't be celebrating this benevolent year.

You'd prefer the whole thing just be calm.
But the repeater hasn't been invented:
once happened, erased from the future.

As the slap calls out from the backside
you think it's a two year old being trained for the future.
But the future is just being invented. It's calm.

Danko's Nudie Suit

Oh Nudie, I didn't know you cut
Danko a suit. The vest is listed as missing,

stolen from an egg shell Malibu wall.
I'd like to think I could walk it out

but Rick Danko was slim in 1975
white leather smoke along some Malibu wall,

some sunset, some Zuma,
the white sand skin, make what you want

of the scenery. Oh Nudie—roses, roses, simply.
No *Grievous Angel* embroidery

with *the* marijuana, *the* women, and *the* pills.
Nudie, I didn't see those blue stars.

Waylon

It's the third hole, it's the fourth hole—
Waylon Jennings sings as a truck
drives to the Franklin Valley Golf Course.

There's a long spray of slide guitar
and the sunlight is setting on the workday
and God thanks his lucky stars for the songwriter.

But it's not only Nashville songwriters—
there's the player who leaves the holes
the way sun cracks through a cloudy day

as the last pebble is cleared from the truck
and there are no lyrics and no guitar.
The kick and snare and bass set the course

for an outro, an extended chorus—
the bread and butter for a songwriter.
So for this take, no pedal steel guitar,

only a lyric, but somehow the song feels whole.
No one has yet to drive a pickup truck
onto a fresh water beach for the day.

In a think tank the word of the day
is iodine. How could something red cure us?
How can we still drive brown trucks?

But what of the young songwriter?
Is his only instrument the guitar?
A piano would be more wholesome.

But what of the sound from F-holes—
the air moving, made of night and day,
over the strings of the guitar?

All of the voices sing the chorus
in a way only the songwriter
could have imagined—granted, truckless.

Waylon wasn't even all truck stop.
A Cricket, he fell into the country hole
and wasn't always the songwriter

but his persona was the persona that day—
a vocalist and a spare guitar player.
He had the hillbillies singing the chorus.

Many a songwriter with no truck
would see the hole in the guitar
as a pit to the workaday curse.

Sawtooth

The American River can take a body—we skirt it looking for an afternoon, pulling the Jeep onto the sand bar, swimming in cutoffs. There's no reason to worry. The sun is brighter here than anywhere and I am done hurting. Baby, I had a hard time leaving and there are songs to say such things. My mistake was to cross a road so unencumbered with pay phones. I couldn't reach you when I most needed to and so here I am new to the lost coast. I know what you look like should you give up and chase me, or if I give up and chase back to you. Foolishness happens in small moments and true fools act on those moments. In the thick band, we were lovers. But lovers seems so kiss-proof and untouchable. No one would have a problem kissing us or talking. The brave thing would be delivering us from north and south. I've given *Second Helping* another listen and am suddenly loving the amber bend in the squirrel's tail. I've met new people—friends are never far. Short on hard drugs, we mostly chase this river.

Cato

Like truly old-fashioned rabbit ears
I'd stretched my vocabulary.

One guy was interested in racing, said
these hills would be good for testing corners,

for taking an advanced test.
I told him, Music has been lost to the war,

clashing with models is my new love.
I clash with them until their lungs give out

and their arms split like swans, trying
before finding flight. When they hover

water falls from their tails and you say,
This is not magic. Scuffing around the island

cigarette ashes belong to the wind
as the guests dip into their skiffs.

A crowd sometimes presents a vacancy—
time enough to poach something in olive oil.

Inviting guests to the hermit's cabin
when not the hermit, you feel the cuckoo.

Entertaining is not a right but a feeling
like pride, like glitter humping in some unused room.

The King boys had a carport sort of like this.
They had a grandpa with a hillbilly zoo.

He was departed-Amish and so shunned.
One late summer day I walked over

to find two baby black bear. They were
like those furry worms as they slid

on the slick and gray concrete.
Most people are able to care for themselves.

Most people know how to leave.
For *me* the ocean's black is always there.

Acknowledgements:

Thanks to the editors of the following journals where these poems first appeared:

Black and Grey Magazine:	"Hackleshin Road"
Ellipsis:	"Tranquility Pike"
Forklift, Ohio:	"These States"
The Hat:	"Class of '96"
Heavy Feather Review:	"Measley Ridge Road," "Tennyson Road," "Zahn's Corner Road"
Shampoo:	"Retrospective"
Sonora Review:	"Alaskan Abecedary"
Spinning Jenny:	"Red Hollow Road," "Shyville Road"
Tampa Review:	"Our Ántonia"
Quarterly West:	"Rodeo Ramble"
Wicked Alice:	"Poem of the Teenager"
Word For / Word:	"Chenoweth Fork Road," "Cove Road," "Union Hill Road."

I'd like to thank my teachers: John Drury, Jim Cummins, Jeredith Merrin, Don Bogen, and the late David Citino. I would also like to acknowledge the support of various kinds from dear friends: Jeff Butler, Mary Lou Buschi, Justin Preston, Richard Lucas, Byron Bailey, Hannah Reck, Sophia Kartsonis, Kevin Oberlin, Matthew Aquilone, Kristi Maxwell, Cindy King, and Michael Rerick. I am forever grateful to Jared Michael Wahlgren for taking on this coast, and to Kyle McCord and Nick Courtright for shepherding. I'd like to thank my CCAD colleagues and students as well as my grand and cavernous family—most of all, my lovely, hard-working, sharp-witted parents, John and Virginia. And Lesley, these poems are better for your guidance. We have new work to attend to—much greater.

About the Author:

Joshua Butts is from Jackson, OH. He received a B.A. and an M.A. from The Ohio State University and a PhD from the University of Cincinnati, where he was a Charles Phelps Taft Dissertation Fellow. His poems have appeared in various journals including *Sonora Review*, *Tampa Review, Harpur Palate*, *Forklift, Ohio*, and *Quarterly West*. Butts is currently a Visiting Professor of English and Philosophy at the Columbus College of Art and Design. He lives in Columbus, OH with his wife Lesley Jenike and daughter Willa Mae.